" Stigma"

By: Earselean C.

Authors Biography

My name is Earselean. I am also known as "Tootie" by my family. But, in the professional world, I am known as Earselean.

I have always been inspired to write. I started writing as a child in a journal at 10 years old. That journal was a life-saving thing for me because it allowed me to express how I felt, and the only other person who knew what I was writing was the good Lord. It was a tool that my counselor suggested I should use when I felt overwhelmed and anxious about life.

I am grateful for the instinct to write. I was told in college that I was a great writer. I have written so many journals that I should have over 20 books published. However, I never looked at myself as an author.

This is my second book. Telling the truth about my feelings, and what I am dealing with in life is therapy for me.

Chapter 1.

It started when I was very young.

I believe I started feeling things, and seeing things, at 3-years-old or so. I remember being young and drinking a cup of water and seeing things at the bottom of the cup. It looked like radio TC playing. I showed my mother but she didn't see anything. I could write a whole book about mental illness and PTSD.

However, I feel like that is not representing the full scale of what is going on with myself and others dealing with the STIGMA. So, here we are discussing a known topic that is shamed on, or mostly taboo to speak of. Mental illness... Whether you are Bi-polar, Depressed, Anxious, Psychotic, etc.

I went a few years without having any incidents. However, when I was around 20 years old, something happened. I remember going to beauty college, working full-time, having a new husband, a new baby, and I broke. My mind began to race, to run from me. I used to wonder, what is going on with me? Going to work scared me, driving scared me, going to class scared me. I lived in total fear that something horrible was going to happen to me.

Chapter 1 continued.

I was in class and I heard that my cousin had been shot in the face. I broke... I became overwhelmed with fear. We attended church on Sundays, and learned bible study, attended youth meetings, junior mission meetings, and BTU (Bible Training Union)... I did not understand why the topic, and more help, was not available to people in the church.

As I tried to work, I would sit there, staring into space. I worked in a manufacturing plant. As I soldered, my mind would drift off to deep, deep thoughts of death and destruction. I was so scared.

When I drove my car, I felt like someone was after me or someone was trying to harm me. It was bad. If it started raining, I became extremely scared, and immediately wanted to go home. When I got home, I wanted to hide. I wanted to hide in the closet or under the bed. Everything that happened around me was scary, and I did not know why.

I didn't want to admit to anyone what was going on with me. My aunt, one day at lunch, asked me if I was OK. I said yes, but inside, I was terrified.

Chapter 2.

It was right after my uncle passed away suddenly that I snapped. That was the time I stopped doing what other people thought I should be doing and began to live my life being free of being told what to do and bossed around.

I wanted to be a business owner. I wasn't scared of that. Yes! The thought of failure did exist, but I always had faith.

It was 1997. It was time to get better. I scheduled to see a psychiatrist. I knew that a regular doctor was going to tell me that was what I needed to do.

I went to see the doctor and told him everything that I had gone through as a child, and everything that I was currently experiencing in my life with the anxiousness, and the innate fear of harm with no apparent reason for harm to exist in my life. I was so glad that I did not have to go around and around with my health insurance carrier (UNC) at the time. I would have lost it if I had done. I went straight in to see the doctor without a referral.

The doctor that basically saved my life prescribed me Lorazepam and Clonazepam. These two medications worked together in the same family of Xanex. I took clonazepam every day before I started my day and Lorazepam at night before I went to sleep. The best relief in medicine, I thought.

I began to regain my strength and confidence in my dreams and goals in life. I stayed on this medication for a couple of years until I became pregnant with my second son. It seemed like things were OK. I did not, and had not, experienced the tenseness again. However, I started to experience panic and anxiety attacks.

Now, this was totally a new experience to me because every time there was any type of panic, death in the family, or crisis, I would tense up and my chest would hurt. There was shooting pain in my arms, and I could not sleep. I started seeing an MD. I knew what would get me some relief. The Lorazepam... He did not know anything about the Clonazepam. I knew exactly what medication I was takingback in 1997. It was now 2002, and all hell had broken loose in my life.

Chapter 3.

My husband was cheating on me, and my finances were in ruin. There was nothing that I could do. So, because I wanted him gone, I filed for bankruptcy.

He returned home to me and the kids, as I have mentioned. This cycle of frustration is explained in my last novel (Healing from Trauma and Abuse). My mental state was unknown, and it felt weird to me. It felt weird because, again, whenever something would change in my life - good or bad - it started to be harder to adjust. My chest would pound, I could not breath, and I felt faint-ish. The hospital was my second home. I had many tests run, much medicine was tried, and every test came back normal. I was then diagnosed with severe depression.

I was like, what is severe depression? Why? How? I was introduced to Zoloft, Prozac, Paxil. You name it, I was on it, trying to alleviate this empty feeling on the inside of me.

Chapter 4.

The medicines had so many side effects: dry mouth, restlessness, hunger, anger, moodiness, diarrhea, headaches, leg aches. It seemed like the medicine was making me feel even more frustrated. I began drinking to get sleep. I did it often. Beer was my choice. The antidepressants did not work for me.

My father called me one day and asked me if I had ever been diagnosed with being bi-polar. I said no. I often had been told that manic depression is a form of bi-polar. But I had not been diagnosed. My father has depression and has had it for most of his life. He turned to alcohol and drugs. I have never been a drug person, nor a hard alcohol type of person. So, he told me to watch out for it.

I knew most of my mother's side of the family was mentally ill, too. So, how could I escape it?

By this point, we'd had our last child, and shortly after that I realized - hey, I am not living...

Chapter 5.

I moved to a small town to get away from the everyday struggle of working at a regular job, and not feeling fulfilled. My ex-husband moved on with his mistress, and I came to find out that her son was having an identity crisis. My sons had to go over to their father's house to visit, and there was nothing that I could do about it. I went into total panic mode. I was already depressed, and the medicine had not worked in years, so I ended up in hospital for 3 straight days. I'll never forget; it was the same day Whitney Houston died in 2012.

I could not handle that shock, and the fact that my children may be at risk from a person I thought of at the time as a predator. It all added to my anxiety. I was crippled by fear. It made me wonder, why are things this way? But then I think about my childhood, and how traumatic it was. That was why I suffered. Moving forward, I was prescribed more anti-depressant drugs that helped - but I would not stay on them. As soon as I felt better, I would stop taking them.

Chapter 6.

Staying on medication even after feeling better was hard. My mind couldn't handle stress. I eventually moved back to our hometown. The children were more comfortable being near their friends back home. I managed to stay away from anti-depressants for three years.

In 2015, I was leaving a bad relationship that was toxic. The guy, I believe, was going through some mental things as well. He lied a lot, cheated, manipulated situations, womanized, and had a lot of anger stored up inside of him. I feel that caused a lot of his issues, and my issues caused me to attract him. I was dealing with abandonment issues which caused me to be in bad situations that were not good for me, no matter what.

My self-esteem was low, and depression did not make it any better. I started feeling those low feelings again, and I could not manage them. I went to see my doctor and took some time off of work to get better.

I know when I am not feeling well. Growing up the way I did triggered a lot of these feelings. The psychiatrist prescribed medication, and he would talk to me a little bit. The medication that he put me on was like an instant happy pill. The pill made me sleep, and I did not feel any type of sorrow. It made me eat a lot, though, and I began to gain weight as I started to live my life again.

After about four weeks of treatment, I began to start hanging out with friends and learned to love myself more. I did not worry about not having a man, nor did I worry about what the man did to break my heart. It was rough. I had breakups from time to time. I dealt with abandonment issues along with all the anticipation of something horrible was going to happen.

After all, that is what I was exposed to. It caused me to love the wrong people. It is important in life that you learn to love yourself. If you do not love yourself, you will continue to try to please people, and people will run all over you. You have to love yourself, and forgive mostly, in order to move on. Not for other people but for you.

Chapter 7.

- It was found that most people in the US choose not to talk about mental illness and its effects on their lives. The illnesses that I am mostly referring to in this novel are depression, panic attacks, anxiety attacks, pain in legs, stress, jolts in your sleep, and being constantly afraid of the worst.

- My definition of depression is: your lowest point in life, a feeling of worry, Fatigue. MD states that feelings of severe despondency and dejection are common. (Oxford Dictionary)

- Fatigue is extreme tiredness resulting from mental or physical exertion or illness.

  Worry: give way to anxiety or unease; allow one's mind to dwell on difficulty or troubles.

Continued Chapter 7.

Stress: Stress generally refers to two things: the psychological perception of pressure, on the one hand, and the body's response to it, on the other, which involves multiple systems, from metabolism to muscles to memory.

Stress is necessary for all living systems; it is the means by which they encounter and respond to the challenges and uncertainties of existence. The perception of danger sets off an automatic response system, known as the fight-or-flight response, that, activated through hormonal signals, prepares an animal to meet a threat or to flee from it. (Psychology Today)

Chapter 8.

(PTSD) (Depression) (Panic and Anxiety)

Getting to the underlining cause of depression can be tricky. It was something that I did not really care to talk about with random folks. I was afraid of being judged. My mother use to say mean things like, "girl, you better go get on that medication that you take". Which she did this, she often accused me of being on drugs and alcohol, too.

That was not true. Many people suffer from anxiety, but often, it goes untreated. Anxiety impacts 18.1% of adults in the United States. Furthermore, it's estimated that 31.1% of adults in the U.S. have had an anxiety disorder at some point in their lives. Anxiety is more common among women, at 23.4%, compared to men at 14.3%. Even though anxiety can be treatable, only 36.9% seek help. (Mindful Searching 2020)

Chapter 9.

I'm happy that I listen to my body, and do not live by the stigmatization of what society thinks of as being normal and abnormal. I always have thought outside of the box, and I encourage my children to do the same. Let no-one set limits for you and tell you what you cannot do. As of today, I am 45 years old and have lived with the disease since I was 20 years old. I am grateful to have a better understanding about what is going on with me, and I will let no one else's opinions dictate what I should feel, or say, to the contrary of depression.

The effects that it has had on my life - no one else has any idea. I know that most of the depression is caused by circumstances. Since I know this, I am cautious about who I allow in my life. If you are not here to help me be better or grow then you are not allowed in my space.

Chapter10.

Growth and well-being is a lifestyle for me; it is a way of being and living. I have to be healthy in order to mentor, train my employees, and teach my grandchildren better. I have to be conscious of my surroundings - of what I see and hear. It all affects me. I'm sensitive to stress and allergic to drama. However, through the years, it all has managed to find me.

My father once told me, "You are a glutton for punishment, aren't you?" He knows all so well about mental illness, for he is a diagnosed schizophrenic, alcoholic, manic depressive, and has PTSD.

I don't believe that you are or should be going off of what a lot of doctors say unless you have been with the same physician for many years. This is just my opinion. I am not a doctor, counselor, or licensed therapist. I just feel like folks are on medication that they don't need. When a person is always switching doctors, I feel like the relationship is unknown. A new doctor, new medication. It may even start an entirely different problem!

This is why my doctor always asks me, "How do you feel?" This is where there is genuine concern for the patient comes into it. Not just handing out medications. I'm talking about taking care of mentally ill people.

I don't consider myself as mentally ill. I consider myself as a person who has been traumatized and shocked throughout life. I am working hard to overcome my challenges and become a better version of myself.

If I find myself becoming stressed, I go for a walk or exercise. This helps circulate my blood and helps clear the mind. I recently started meditating, too. This calms the mind. I practice it for about 5-10 minutes a day. Controlling the mind. Oftentimes, when stress takes over our lives, we want a quick fix, and often all that is needed is the calming of the mind.

I came back from the Army back in 1998 because we had started field exercises. The exercises involved blowing up territories. This was all training. But it still felt like a war zone. I was suffering from PTSD (Post-Traumatic Stress Disorder). Most people who have been in war zones or highly violent situations for a long period of time experience this.

My life was like a war zone as a child. I had to become an adult at an early age. It wasn't my choice, but I had to step up to protect myself, my brother, and my siblings. That was not a fun time for me. But, through it all, I learned something. I learned strength, courage, resilience, and patience, and no amount of medication can teach a person that. Once I started living again, my emotions balanced out. I began to experience a new way of life for myself. I started living, breathing the fresh air, enjoying the fine foods that I enjoy so much, and I traveled. It all made me feel like I was being the adult that I aspired to be, and not having anyone to be responsible for but myself. Yes, I was raising 3 sons at the time. But when they would go over to their grandmother's house, or to their father's for the weekend, I spent time loving and appreciating myself.

On the weekends, I'd go to resorts, and bars to just relax in the lime light of high profile people. It's important to know yourself, love yourself, and get to know yourself. I have to know how I am feeling and why I am feeling this or that way.

Mornings were crucial for me, and when I finished working in the evening were also important times. It was important that I took this time out when my children were busy to gain focus on myself.

I wanted to address mental illness because data stats show that one of the main causes of homelessness, drug abuse, and alcohol abuse is mental illness. Society has not done enough to protect those who are affected with a disorder.

Chapter 11.

According to the most recent annual survey by the U.S. Conference of Mayors, major cities across the country report that top causes of homelessness among families were: (1) lack of affordable housing, (2) unemployment, (3) poverty, and (4) low wages, in that order.42 The same report found that the top four causes of homelessness among unaccompanied individuals were (1) lack of affordable housing, (2) unemployment, (3) poverty, (4) mental illness and the lack of needed services, and (5) substance abuse, and the lack of needed services. Tischler, et al. explain that Mothers experiencing homelessness: mental health, support and social care needs, 15 Health Soc. Care Community 3, 246-253);

It's really sad. It is! Why is it taboo to talk about mental illness and the effects it has on society?

For one thing, it's embarrassing. Most folks don't want to admit that they're having a mental crisis. Secondly, where are the local resources, and how do you get access to them?

I remember when I was having a nervous breakdown. My family had fallen apart, my finances were destroyed, and my husband had left me for another woman. I broke! I spent relentless hours on the phone trying to get advice about what I was feeling and the next steps to take. I was literally having a meltdown. I called one hotline, wasa transferred to another hotline, then to a voicemail that told me to call another number. I was like, huh? This is supposed to be helping? This was a joke!

No wonder suicide rates are through the roof. Currently, here in 2020, the world is experiencing a pandemic. It is advised that people don't leave their homes unless they are wearing a face mask. You must use hand sanitizer after every public transaction. Folks are losing their minds in their homes and on their jobs. The country is in a bad state of being. Suicide is the nation's 10th-leading cause of death with 14.2 deaths per 100,000 people, though that rate alone belies the scope of the problem. While thousands of people die by suicide each year, millions think about it. In 2017, 10.6 million American adults seriously

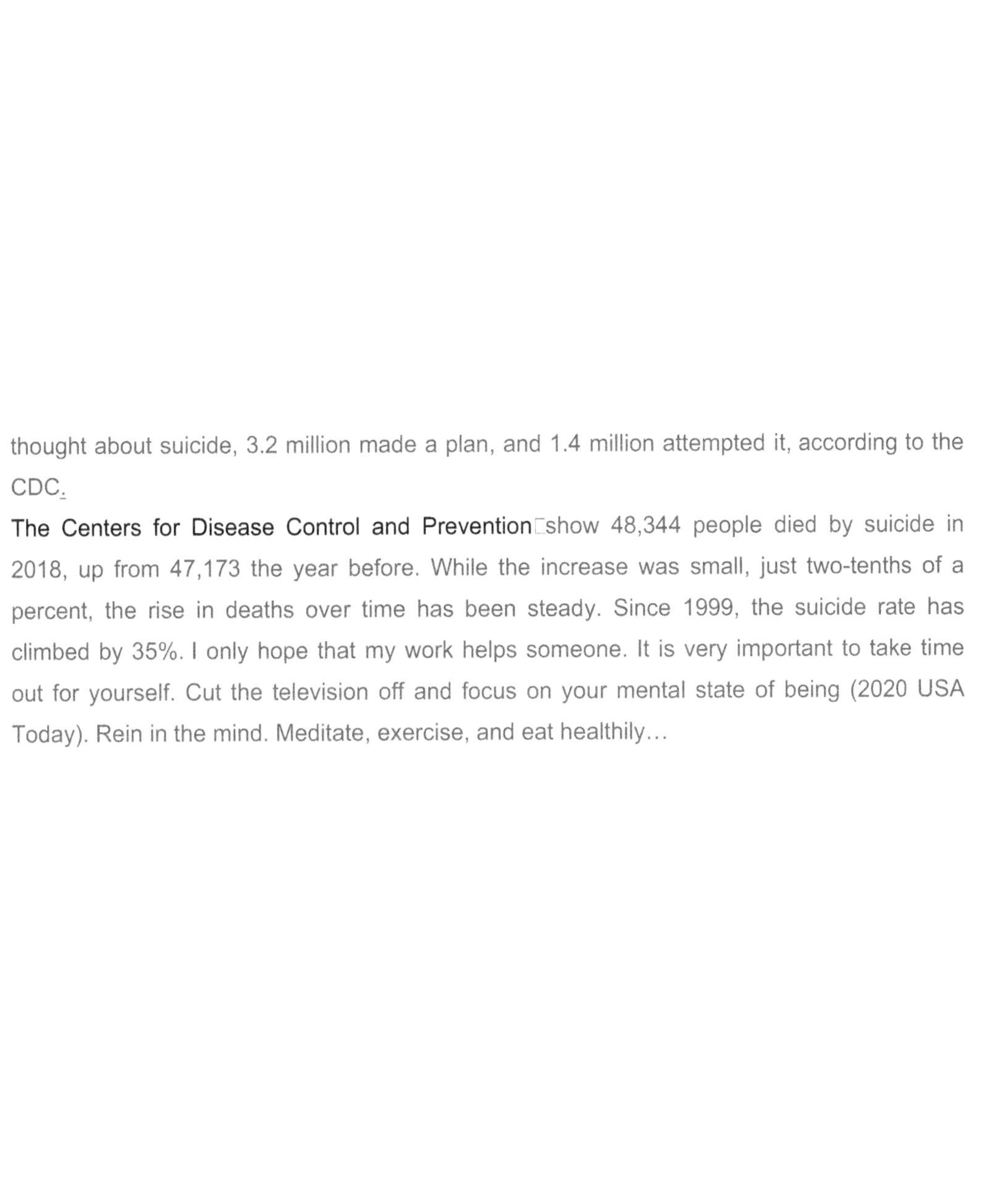

thought about suicide, 3.2 million made a plan, and 1.4 million attempted it, according to the CDC.

The Centers for Disease Control and Prevention show 48,344 people died by suicide in 2018, up from 47,173 the year before. While the increase was small, just two-tenths of a percent, the rise in deaths over time has been steady. Since 1999, the suicide rate has climbed by 35%. I only hope that my work helps someone. It is very important to take time out for yourself. Cut the television off and focus on your mental state of being (2020 USA Today). Rein in the mind. Meditate, exercise, and eat healthily…

Chapter 12.

Being depressed is horrible. Depression itself takes a lot of energy from a person. I remember working at an insurance company, and there was a woman who worked with me. She would always be depressed, which caused her to miss work, and when she was in work she would be alone a lot.

She was on my team, so I saw her moods daily. I was the team leader at the time, and what I did was empathize with her. I decided one day to talk to her and see how she was feeling. She would tell me how she and her mother did not get along, how her boyfriend at the time was in and out of jail, and that all made her depressed. The people around her helped her as much as they could but, she never could seem to bounce back from her depression. She said she was on medication but did not like taking her medicine.

The medication made her feel worse. I could relate to this; my depression was circumstantial.

 The illness would cause her to stay at home more often and miss lots of work. Eventually, this caused her to get laid off from work.

That was the dilemma. Most folks who are experiencing the stigma of depression or PTSD don't really want to take the medication. The medication has too many side effects. Also, a person doesn't want to feel trapped by medication and its dependency. I remember asking the doctor, if you put me on anti-depressants will I have to remain on them for the rest of my life?

Chapter 13.

The answer was, well, we will have to see how you do. I must say that I have been battling depression and anxiety since I was 20 years old. I know that my anxiety has affected my relationships because I am not really capable of holding together romantic relationships. The fear of loss causes me to grasp on tight and they pull away. Sometimes, I will sabotage the relationship myself, unaware that I was doing it. It is now that I am deliberately working on myself and loving all of me, now that I have seen this pattern. Since my divorce, certain things in a relationship I could not tolerate; I couldn't even imagine me being in a happy place. I feel it is important to spend the time alone and with people you love who understand the divorce process.

Now that I have come to love and listen to my gut, heart, mind, and spirit, I know what I want from a partner. One of the things that I have found useful to me is meditation. I learned this technique while talking to my middle son. He had mentioned that he was going to start meditating. He had just broken up with his girlfriend, and he wanted to calm his mind.

Six months later, I went through a breakup. It was after three years of being with a toxic person. I sat down, Indian-style, on my living room floor, palms up, and I turned on meditation music. Soft water flowing music; vibrations are some good starting places. The key is to breath in deep, and exhale. Breath in deep, and exhale out. I do this five times a session. This calms the mind and helps relax you while you are listening to the sound of waves.

I have practiced being hypnotized. This felt great to experience the drifting off to sleep lightly, and your mind is focused on the energy around you. Energy is flowing through you, and it feels light. The amount of time that I spend trying to conquer anxiety and panic attacks. It helps.

I started to experience jolts. While I was sleeping, I was jerking. This was me having these panic and anxiety attacks while I was asleep. I had no control of what my brain was doing while I was sleeping. I just knew that the jolts would wake me up. Some nights, I would not get any sleep at all. It was astonishing.

I conquered the anxiety through monitoring what I drank or ate before bed and the amount of caffeine intake at night, as well as keeping an eye on the amount of stress that I observed (via news, social media, and phone conversations).

The meditating usually lasted anywhere between 15-30 minutes. It would depend on how much I needed to relax. This was, and still is, something that helps me with my anxiety and panic attacks. It is important to get the body in check and calm it down. Having so much anxiety and panic can, over time, cause high-blood pressure, sleep deprivation, mood swings, over eating, under eating, etc…

Chapter 14.

I wrote this book because I have dealt with a lot in my life. Certain things cannot be undone.

I used to internalize things, and the result was depression. Depression is like a cold. Anxiety is like the cough that comes with the cold; panic is like the sneezing that comes with the cold. Depression is the diagnosis. Anxiety, and panic are the symptoms of the diagnosis.

I do the best I can to keep my stress low, and moderate. I don't like stress or arguing at this point in my life. I used to, and that helped prolong the healing with my depression.

Exercise is a great tool for easing anxiety. I started walking 2 miles a day on the treadmill. This worked out for me, too. For the most part, I have figured out how to manage the symptoms of the diagnosis.

The STIGMA in talking about such a topic exist because, so many people fear how they will be judged.

People feel that they are misunderstood, or people will think they are crazy. Many people suffer from depression for many reasons. It is best to see a doctor.

If you are like me, and you have tried the medications, therapy sessions, and nothing has worked, then try meditation and calming the mind. The mind has a lot of things to process on a daily basis. So, sub-consciously, we are doing and feeling things that internalize. Once that happens, get ready for the PTSD, depression, anxiety, and a host of other things that our mind takes in.

Chapter 15.

The other case that I witnessed was my own brother. He is 46 years old now and his mental capacity has dropped very low. He is diagnosed as being mentally retarded. He takes the higher caliber drugs like Seroquel, Trazodone, Lorazepam, and a host of others. This medication is used to treat certain mental/mood conditions (such as schizophrenia, bipolar disorder, sudden episodes of mania or depression associated with bipolar disorder).

Quetiapine is known as an anti-psychotic drug. It is in place to keep him calm. He also has multiple personalities. He has about 5 different people that his personality portrays.

For the most part, the medication keeps him calm. He loves music and laughing. He watches television and understands what is going on in the show he is watching.

But he can be a very angry person when he is not on his medicine. He will hit and use profanity.

For the most part, he can be handled. But sometimes, he has to be handled by people who won't give in to him. He won't be a part of this study. But it is one way to show mental illness in the family.

So, the question that is left is - did I get this from my family genes or did this come from traumatic experiences?

Chapter 16.

My father was diagnosed as mentally ill. He accepts it is what it is, and tries to live life as normally as possible.

Over the last nine years or so, I have been able to recognize patterns within myself. This is what lets me know that something is not feeling right or is off somewhere.

My mom and her husband helped me with my children after I went through the divorce, and while I was trying to figure life out without my ex-husband. They would keep the kids at the weekend, during the summer, and over school breaks.

All of the kids wanted to be at their grandmother's house. It was the thing they loved. I spent a lot of that time soaking. I'd go to work in the salon, and get my supper after work, go home to watch television, and sleep. That was my life. The "STIGMA". No one wanted to know or even asked me how I felt, now that I was raising 3 sons alone.

I dated different men. But I would always find a way to sabotage the good guys, and keep the bad guys around.

Over time, though, through trial and error, I realized I had to learn. If I didn't, it was going to cost me my life - depressed or not. I was trying to run from my illness. I didn't talk about it a lot. I just dealt with what I could and how I could on a day-to-day basis. So, if I didn't feel like going to work, I went. If I didn't feel like cooking, I did. I found a way to work it off or play it through. Something like a mantra - let the emotions pass over me.

One doctor asked me, years ago, how I managed that suffering. I told her, "the best way I could". It does not feel good to talk to people who do not know how you feel. They project their issues over to you, and they tell you this without knowing what/how to feel. Mental illness has nothing to do with logic. It is the chemical imbalance in the brain that causes these onsets of emotions.

The fits of crying, darkness, negative thinking, introversion. One of the other ways I could escape from these internal feelings was to leave. I'd go stay with a friend for a few days, visit a fantastic resort, drink the finest wines, dance, and spend time loving me again. Oftentimes, when I started feeling low, I would take it as the universe saying that I needed to love myself more and be around things that I love. Which was food, sex, and Brazilian jazz.

It felt weird, being misunderstood while I was sick. When I would go through the highs and lows of depression, some would even say it was manic depression. Bipolar disorder.

Yep, that is definitely a no-no to talk about. My community would judge me so horrifically. I just didn't bother. Maybe I judged myself? Instead, I'd go to the doctor, and let him/her give me something to calm my nerves, or whatever I was feeling at the time. Sometimes, all I needed was a good conversation.

I have always been smart and resourceful. I'd just gone through a lot early in life.

Chapter 17.

That traumatized me. I'm older now, and so I can share with my readers what it is feels like to be misunderstood, and to never be ashamed of how you feel. Don't act out of character. I've done that before. Cussing people out, down talking people, and sabotaging a great relationship. All of this time, I was learning how to treat myself, love myself, and to handle these emotions from my chemical imbalance.

I told my sons that I wanted to tell them about my illness once they became a certain age. I just haven't done so yet. I feel that I am going to conquer a lot still in life. I believe in the Universe and asking for what I want through faith. I still watch my actions, though, because I don't want to act in mania.

I recently learned that writing is my passion along with helping people with their shortcomings. I have always been the type of person in school who accepted the rejects. I felt I could help them be a better person. Whether it was getting clothes for them, getting the most popular guy's attention, or wearing the latest hairstyle. I would help.

If you ever find yourself wondering or feeling weird for a period of time, it would be of interest to see a doctor. I had to handle my feelings alone. That is never a good place to be. One should not have to suffer in silence. I challenge anyone who is reading this novel to get help.

Chapter 18.

Talk to someone you can trust. It will only benefit you in the long term. It isn't everyone's business to judge you for something you cannot control.

Don't do drugs of any kind. Don't consume too much alcohol to ease the sorrow. Alcohol is a depressant and will make you feel worse.

Once you have gone through your therapy, my hope is that you start your own journal and keep up with your journey. Dealing with depression hasn't been easy. But I managed to cope and use the resources that were available to me.

As I have mentioned before, about 18% of our population experience some sort of mental difficulty. Sometimes, it is manageable, and sometimes it is an ongoing battle for life.

I remember when I was 25. I asked Dr. Stephens if I would deal with depression for the rest of my life, and he told me that it was possible that I would. From that point on, I made a decision to monitor my feelings. I decided that the illness would not control me. If I needed medication to sleep, to cope for a while, then so be it. I had worked externally, and internally, on myself to feel better.

Chapter 19.

I was glad to know that celebrities started to open up about the illness. Our late Abraham Lincoln was ill with depression. He called it his dark days – and that is exactly how it feels.

Dwayne Johnson stated that depression never discriminates. He tweeted later, "Took me a long time to realize it but the key is to not be afraid to open up. Especially us dudes have a tendency to keep it in. You're not alone." (Web MD 2020)

I don't know about guys but I do have three sons so I will be watching them. I really want to know if the illness is genetic in my immediate family or if it's circumstantial.

Lady Gaga says she has been dealing with the illness her entire life. I really felt this one because I realized I suffered from it (depression) when I was 20 years old. I'm 45 years old now. And I deal with the illness on and off still. Lady Gaga said she thinks it's important for people to talk about their mental health.

"If we share our stories and stick together, we're stronger." (Web MD 2020) I totally agree. This is why I am speaking of the illness.

I feel that it is important to speak out. I remember reading that one actor stated that he thinks society finds it more acceptable to admit to a drug problem than clinical depression.

That is a problem. I feel like and this is my opinion. Why would society like or have more empathy towards a person with a drug problem rather than a person suffering with mental illness?

We lost Robin Williams to the illness. In 2006, he described his highs and lows to (NPR) Terry Gross. "Do I perform sometimes in a manic style? Yes. Am I manic all the time? No. Do I get sad? Oh yeah. Does it hit me hard? Oh yeah." (Web MD 2020)

So, you see, depression, anxiety, and mental illness do not discriminate. It is something that can be managed. Every day it changes, whether it will be for better or worse. If you push through for just one more day, you'll get another day to deal with the illness and work completely on yourself. I will list a few hot-lines to help with your struggle; a few places that have helped me in my area with my struggle. You will beat the illness. Continue to be strong.

BetterHelp

990 Villa Street,
Mountain View, CA 94041

contact@betterhelp.com

Mental Help. Net
 1-800-799-4889

Crisis Text Line
 Text HOME to 741741

I hope this helps. I am not a doctor, psychiatrist, or therapist. I just know how I feel when dealing with depression over the years, and I feel that the message, treatment, and symptoms should be openly shared.

EC

www.ingramcontent.com/pod-product-compliance
Lightning Source LLC
Chambersburg PA
CBHW050802240726
48654CB00008B/596